MISGUIDED PASSIONS &

the Lord's Prayer

Endorsements

"IN *MISGUIDED PASSIONS AND THE Lord's Prayer*, Curt Richards examines this message by carefully dissecting the Lord's Prayer and relating it to real-life scenarios. The story starts with a man being tempted to steal and gradually getting enticed to steal more because of the feeling of "false pleasure" in it. In his book, he discusses how these behaviors influence our emotions, creating an uncontrollable passion that leads to sin. This uncontrollable passion is very toxic, and the roots of addiction come about from sin, including any possible mental health issues of the individual.

Curt's book provides an accurate insight into the Bible, breaking down the Lord's Prayer and dissecting every line to its meaning. He gives the reader a better breakdown and grasp of God's plan and purpose and our duty to evangelize the gospel to the unsaved. I endorse Curt's work and look forward to one day having the opportunity to ask questions and learn more about the details of the Bible."

—Robert Cooper
secondary science instructor
Houston, Texas

"I REALLY ENJOYED READING THIS book and would recommend this book for everyone to read—it brought the Lord's Prayer to life. Curt Richards does this by not only providing historical connections but also aligning the message of the Lord's Prayer to our time. In addition, Curt breaks the prayer into parts, which gives an in-depth insight into its meaning. This is an easy-to-read book that gives a feeling of comfort."

—Dr. Natasha Cox-Magno

MISGUIDED PASSIONS &

the Lord's Prayer

CURT RICHARDS

AMBASSADOR INTERNATIONAL
GREENVILLE, SOUTH CAROLINA & BELFAST, NORTHERN IRELAND

www.ambassador-international.com

MISGUIDED PASSIONS AND THE LORD'S PRAYER
©2024 by Curt Richards
All rights reserved

ISBN: 978-1-64960-436-1, paperback
eISBN: 978-1-64960-484-2

Cover Design by Karen Slayne
Interior Typesetting by Dentelle Design
Edited by Terri Hucks

All Scriptural quotations are taken from The King James Version of the Bible. Public Domain.

Ambassador International titles may be purchased in bulk for education, business, fundraising, or sales promotional use. For information, please email sales@emeraldhouse.com.

AMBASSADOR INTERNATIONAL	AMBASSADOR BOOKS
Emerald House	The Mount
411 University Ridge, Suite B14	2 Woodstock Link
Greenville, SC 29601	Belfast, BT6 8DD
United States	Northern Ireland, United Kingdom
www.ambassador-international.com	www.ambassadormedia.co.uk

The colophon is a trademark of Ambassador, a Christian publishing company.

This book is dedicated to my wonderful mother and father, who are now enjoying eternal rest. Thank you for your love and guidance through the years. You are both forever a part of me.

Table of Contents

Author's Note

THE PURPOSE OF THIS BOOK is to unlock the teachings embedded in the Lord's Prayer and to embrace the beautiful words that Jesus spoke. It is my hope that anyone who struggles in the clutches of some unhealthy behavior may find peace and may redirect his misguided passions toward a more fulfilling life.

—Curt Richards

Introduction

A FEW YEARS AGO, I was watching a program on television where I heard a shoplifter speak about his crime. For over a year, he spent every Saturday strolling through the mall, searching for an opportunity to steal. He began with small items and then graduated to larger, more expensive products. He did not need the items he took. Actually, he stored his loot in a rented building and never sold any of his treasures because he was not after money. Stealing gave him the thrill that comes from participating in something that was out of the ordinary. He developed a passion for stealing. This man's passion for life became misguided. He craved excitement in his life and chased the high that came with the act of stealing.

As he was telling his story, his voice cracked with remorse. He felt badly toward the shop owners who had lost merchandise and the patrons who had to pay higher prices because of men like him; but most of all, he regretted his misguided passion. He regretted all the hours spent pursuing an activity that was meaningless and that offered no redeeming value for anyone. Even the high that he received from committing his crime was fleeting.

The time he spent away from his family was not put to any valuable use. This time was lost, never to be recaptured. He could have spent his Saturday afternoons using his time to practice a hobby or learn a skill. He could have taken his children to the zoo or relaxed under a shade tree and read a book. He had passion in his life, but it was misdirected and misguided. This was his greatest regret.

Passions can be positive and enrich your life. Many people have a passion for an art or a sport or helping others. However, sometimes people develop passions that are harmful to themselves and their families. Rarely are these passions planned. They creep into someone's life and slowly build until a breaking point is reached.

When the stresses of life paw at us, we seek comfort. We often run from our problems, only to fall into some compulsive snare. For some people, this behavior manifests itself in the abuse of alcohol or chemicals to deaden the pain, while others develop a preoccupation with food or delve deeply into their work, closing out the world in the name of prosperity. Some turn to gambling, always chasing that elusive "big win"; but they never seem to be satisfied. Still others seek sexual gratification in pornography or in a string of illicit affairs.

We can be drawn into these addictive behaviors because of the effect they have on the emotions. Over time, the behavior becomes an uncontrollable passion because it takes more and more activity to produce the same emotional reward. This is the point at which our lives become misguided. We are completely alone because we never open up to anyone about our problem. If we are a believer, we often turn our face away from God because we do not feel worthy. If we have never experienced God, we refrain from seeking Him; but it is in this darkness that God shines His brightest. This is the time for us to seek Him and pray.

The roots of addiction may stem from mental health issues or some trauma a person has experienced in life. These are problems that are associated with out-of-control feelings and behaviors. Many compulsive and addictive behaviors, such as drug or alcohol dependency, may require professional help. Behavioral counseling coupled with medication, if needed, is only the beginning phase in helping someone through the process of mastering his misguided passion. Success in moving past these behaviors can be attributed to a supportive family and friends as well as to a faith-based life. A loving church family who can understand and provide spiritual guidance is essential for everyone but especially for those who are not fortunate enough to have compassionate people in their lives. When we truly believe in a loving Creator Who wants the best for our lives, we begin to see life on a grand scale. It is only at this point that our individual problems can be put into perspective.

When I was a schoolteacher and needed to explain a difficult concept, I would say to my students, "Please don't hear what I didn't say." They would look bewildered. My meaning was for them *not* to read between the lines and hear something that I was not saying. I wanted them to hear my true message. Because it is easy to insert unstated ideas into someone else's philosophies, I wish to make it very clear what this book is *not* saying. It is not saying that all anyone needs to do is to recite the Lord's Prayer and all will be well in his life. Also, I am not suggesting that someone with a misguided passion needs God more than anyone else. All people need God. The truth is that people in the grip of an addiction or compulsive behavior often feel shamed and judged by others and by God. Because of this feeling of desolation, they find it difficult to reach out for help in achieving a healthy, balanced lifestyle.

In the book of Matthew, where the Lord's Prayer is first recorded, Jesus provides us with a model of how to pray.[1] In this prayer, Jesus is not asking us to live up to a list of moral expectations. He is simply asking us to trust and love God totally. Jesus' words in the Lord's Prayer help us deal with our feelings of loneliness and uproot our fear of being unlovable and unwanted. These words help us open our hearts to a loving God because Jesus is dealing with what is happening in our lives right now, not with the residue of our past.

There is power in the Lord's Prayer, but that power is not in the simple recitation of the words. This prayer is not meant to be used as a charm to ensure good luck or to defeat evil. The Lord's Prayer demonstrates God's power and glory because it is a communication with the living God. The power comes from the heart shift that occurs when we apply these words to our lives.

---

1   Matthew 6:9-13

In the Gospel of Luke, one of Jesus' disciples makes this request: "Lord, teach us to pray."[2] The disciples are not searching for a magical incantation used to ward off life's problems. These disciples are not strangers to prayer. They know many of the Jewish prayers by heart. This disciple is asking for a deeper connection with God. Jesus' words in the Lord's Prayer embody His mission on earth. These words are designed to draw the disciples closer to God and for them to understand this relationship of love.

When we are in the grip of some misguided passion, we despise our actions; yet we cannot imagine ever being free from our bondage. We have a passion for this self-destructive activity; yet we hate ourselves for continuing, leaving us emotionally depleted and feeling like the lowest members of society.

During these times of inner turmoil and unrest, we need to turn to the words of Jesus as He speaks to the Samaritan woman at the well: "Whosoever drinketh of this water shall thirst again: But whosoever drinketh of the water that I shall give him shall never thirst; but the water that I shall give him shall be in him a well of water springing up into everlasting life."[3] Misguided passions do not satisfy. They leave us feeling empty, helpless, yet always thirsty for more. We thirst for something substantial in our lives, yet we feel spiritually drained. We cannot imagine our lives being used to glorify God.

The Samaritan woman is the lowest in her society for several reasons. She is a woman, a second-class citizen. She is a Samaritan,

---

2   Luke 11:1
3   John 4:13-14

despised by the Jews as being an inferior culture. The other women of the village enjoy the company and safety of a group when they draw water. They routinely come together early in the morning to draw their water for the day's chores and to catch up on the latest news of the village. Since this woman comes alone to the well in the middle of the day, she is obviously an outcast. With the exception of the lepers and other afflicted persons, she is the least in her community because she is an adulterer living in sexual sin. She has experienced shame in a very public way.

In Jesus' day, a Samaritan was not considered worthy of sharing a dish or a cup with a Jew. This is probably one of the reasons she is shocked when Jesus asks her for a cup of water. He asks her—a dirty, despicable, sinful Samaritan woman—to use a cup that has been touched by her unclean lips.

Through this encounter with Jesus, the Samaritan woman is changed, and God uses her as a messenger to her people. Jesus gives her an identity and a cause, something that she most likely never dreamed she would ever possess. He sees her as a person of worth. Jesus elevates her out of this dismal place to a position of honor by allowing her to be the first person to whom He openly reveals that He is the Christ. He looks past her misguided passions and gives her life purpose, and the people of her town listen to her when she speaks to them: "Come, see a man, which told me all things that ever I did: is not this the Christ?"[4] Those who heard her went in search of Jesus.

---

4   John 4:29

When we use compulsive behaviors in an attempt to satisfy some emotional thirst, that thirst will never be quenched. Through a relationship with Jesus Christ, we can be used to the glory of the Father, despite how lowly and undeserving we may feel. Our misguided passions can once again be laid straight. Our lives can have purpose in ways we could have only dreamed.

If you look closely at the Lord's Prayer, you will find that it contains the whole of Christianity. If we study the words of Jesus and apply them to our lives, our damaged self-image can be repaired, and the love of God will flow out of us and into others.

Because the Lord's Prayer contains lessons for the whole of life, it is immensely helpful in easing the pain that comes from daily stresses and the fallout of our misguided passions. These words come from Jesus, the Son of God, and they show us the true heart of God. Let us look closely at these beautiful words and see how they can direct our passions and display God's will in our lives.

Our Father which art in heaven, Hallowed be thy name.

Thy kingdom come, Thy will be done in earth, as it is in heaven.

Give us this day our daily bread.

And forgive us our debts, as we forgive our debtors.

And lead us not into temptation, but deliver us from evil: For thine is the kingdom, and the power, and the glory, for ever. Amen.[5]

---

5   Matthew 6:9-13

CHAPTER 1

Our Father

THE WORD "OUR" TELLS US that God is the God of everyone and everything. Too often, we feel so low and so lost and so unworthy that we need to be reminded that our God is the God of all creation and the God of all people. He is the God Who guided Abraham and Moses and is also the same God Who cares for our neighbor and the homeless child. He cares for the forgotten ones, the prisoners, the alcoholics, the food addicts, the pornographers, the workaholics, and anyone whose passions have become misguided.

The phrase "Our Father" indicates the existence of a family with God at its head.

The word used in the Bible for father is *Abba*, which can be closely translated as "Daddy." Jesus is the first to directly address God as Father. In the Old Testament, Abraham acknowledges God as a Father, but he does not directly address God in that manner. In the Gospels of Matthew and Luke, Jesus instructs the disciples and the crowds who have gathered for the Sermon on the Mount to pray to God and to acknowledge Him as "Father." Addressing God in this manner tells us that our Father is approachable. He is not a far-off God who spun the world into existence and left it to run on its own.

The love that a father has for his children shows the fullness of God's love. In the Gospel of Luke, after Jesus has taught the Lord's Prayer to His disciples, He asks them, "If a son shall ask bread of any of you that is a father, will he give him a stone? or if he ask a fish, will he for a fish give him a serpent? Or if he shall ask an egg, will he offer him a scorpion? If ye then, being evil, know how to give good gifts unto your children: how much more shall your heavenly Father give the Holy Spirit to them that ask him?"[1]

By addressing God as Father, we are accepting that we are His children and that we are willing to honor His name. The fifth commandment tells us to "honour [our] father and [our] mother."[2] But how do we honor God? Many would tell us that in order to honor God, we must live our lives pleasing to Him. This is true, but it is misleading. These same people feel that to honor God, we have to be good and follow a list of dos and don'ts. We cannot earn God's love and favor. God's love is a free gift. It is not earned. Shame often keeps us from a full relationship with the Father. The denial we harbor keeps us from accepting the love and favor our Father pours out to us. When we are covered in the shadow of some compulsive behavior, we cry out for God to lift the darkness and wrap His loving arms around us. We crave a loving Father to

---

1   Luke 11:11-13
2   Exodus 20:12

protect us and remove our shame and blanket us with comfort and hope.

God is shrouded in mystery. He is not fully known to us, but the word *Father* helps us feel that we can approach God as a child approaches a loving parent. A child, ashamed of his actions and motives, simply wants to be accepted and to know that he is still loved and that all will be well. This frail child needs to know that his father's hand will pull him into a loving embrace and not be poised over him to strike in anger. The relationship of a father to his children is highly revered by God. God, the Creator of all, chooses the father-child relationship to describe His connection with the human race. This is a deeply personal union.

There are things in our lives that we will share only with our heavenly Father. When we are in the clutches of a misguided passion, we feel isolated from our loved ones. We will not share our weakness with even our closest family and friends. The Heavenly Father's relationship with us is closer than our own earthly father's relationship. We can come to Him and find rest. Because of the acceptance of our Heavenly Father, we can now find the strength to confide in and seek support from trusted friends, family, and counselors.

In Psalm 139, David asks, "Whither shall I go from thy spirit? or whither shall I flee from thy presence? If I ascend up into heaven, thou art there: if I make my bed in hell, behold, thou art there. If I take the wings of the morning, and dwell in the uttermost parts of the sea; Even there shall thy hand lead me, and thy right hand shall hold me."[3] For anyone whose life has been torn by a misguided passion, there is tremendous comfort in knowing that God's love is always present. There is nothing we can do nor anywhere we can go that God's care will not be with us.

CHAPTER 2

Which Art in Heaven

OFTEN, WHEN WE THINK OF Heaven, we imagine a beautiful place, peaceful and serene, where we will have no worries or cares. We yearn for total peace. After we read the Scriptures, we imagine Heaven to be a city with golden streets or mansions unlike any on earth. In our own minds, we may dream of a tranquil lake, bounded by snow-capped mountains or a lush forest carpeted with cool, soft moss. God is there, and so are the loved ones who have gone before us. At least, this is how we might imagine Heaven.

The Bible does speak of Heaven as a place. More than anywhere else in the New Testament, the book of Revelation describes the physical attributes of Heaven. Mostly, we know that it is a place of perfection. Here, God provides perfect fellowship with perfect protection, where all of our needs are met in a perfect way.

In chapter twenty-two of the Gospel of Matthew, Jesus describes Heaven as a banquet, where believers will celebrate with God. In the Gospel of John, Jesus speaks of Heaven being a house with many rooms that He has prepared for His disciples to spend eternity.[1] Rather than concern ourselves with the physical attributes of Heaven, we can consider Heaven as a condition of total and complete communion with God. God is in this situation we call Heaven, and He exists in a state of perfect peace and pure love.

Heaven is not a place for worldly thoughts, deeds, or desires. Jesus makes this clear in Matthew 6: "For where your treasure is, there will your heart be also."[2] When we think of Heaven as a condition of the heart—a place for the soul to rest—we realize that the misguided passions that run our lives do not fit in a Heaven-bound mind.

To pray "Our Father, which art in heaven" is to acknowledge our need for a life where we can control our un-heavenly deeds and desires. It is a place where we are forgiven by God.

When someone's passions become misguided, his life is incomplete. An emptiness exists that needs attention. The void that needs filling is often the catalyst that leads to our misguided passions. Our Father is a Father of completeness. He offers us a way out of the dismal. For the person who has fallen deep into a compulsive behavior, this liberation from the abyss would be a Heavenly experience. Our Father offers us an opportunity to join Him in a Heavenly respite from our shame.

---

1   John 14:2-3
2   Matthew 6:21

CHAPTER 3

Hallowed Be Thy Name

WHEN MOSES ENCOUNTERS GOD IN the desert at Mount Horeb, a personal relationship forms. Before this time, God is often referred to as *El*, but this is not His name; this is a pagan term for any deity. The Scriptures pair *El* with other words to show the nature of God. Some examples are as follows:

- El Shaddai—"God of the mountains"
- El Olam—"God of eternity"
- El Roi—"God Who sees me"

We also see *El* added to the end of words, as in Israel and Bethel; but El is not God's name. God becomes personal when He reveals His name.

When Moses approaches the burning bush, God gives him a commission to bring the Israelites out of Egypt. Moses responds, "Behold, when I come unto the children of Israel, and shall say unto them, The God of your fathers hath sent me unto you; and they shall say to me, What is his name? what shall I say unto them? And God said unto Moses, I Am That I Am: and he said, Thus shalt thou say unto the children of Israel, I Am hath sent me unto you."[1] Names are very personal. God reaches out to humanity and makes a personal connection with His creation when He tells us His name.

God's name, translated into Roman script, is *YHWH*. His name in Hebrew contains no vowels; and for centuries, it was considered blasphemous to utter the name of God; therefore, the exact pronunciation has been lost. The most modern form of His name is *Yahweh*, often rendered *Jehovah* in many texts. The three most popular translations of the Bible (King James, New American Standard, and the New International Version) never use the actual name of God. They substitute *GOD* and *LORD* in all capital letters where *YHWH* should be.

Revealing His name to the human race is the first instance of God's reaching out to all people. This seemingly unapproachable God chooses to become personal and tell us His name. Yahweh, the God that Moses cannot approach on the mountain, is reaching out His holy arm and placing it on our filthy shoulders.

The next instance of God's reaching out to a sinful world with His name is predicted by the prophet Jeremiah: "Behold, the days come, saith the LORD, that I will raise unto David a righteous Branch, and a King shall reign and prosper, and shall execute judgment and justice in the earth. In his days Judah shall be saved, and Israel shall

---

1   Exodus 3:13-14

dwell safely: and this is his name whereby he shall be called, THE LORD OUR RIGHTEOUSNESS."[2]

The Gospel of John begins by referring to Jesus as "the Word." John tells us that Jesus is also God: "In the beginning was the Word, and the Word was with God, and the Word was God. The same was in the beginning with God."[3]

Jesus instructs His disciples to consider God's name as hallowed, or sacred, and to address God as such. Jesus is also teaching that our holy God is accessible to all. If this were not the case, Jesus would not have given us this prayer. He is teaching that even though the hallowed name of God is to be set apart, His love for us is individual and personal.

Our sin is blatantly obvious when contrasted against the pure, hallowed nature of God. As much as it may hurt, this moral inventory is important for us to experience. When we realize the vast chasm that separates our filthy selves from the purity of God, we reach out, yearning to be cleansed. God had a plan from the beginning of creation to offer Himself to a sinful, self-absorbed world. Yahweh closed the gap when He offered His Son as a sacrifice and the Holy Spirit as the Comforter.

When Jesus says, "Believe me that I am in the Father and the Father in me,"[4] He is saying that He is the Embodiment of the Father and that He stands before the world with total authority given to Him from God the Father. This concept is difficult for us to wrap

---

2   Jeremiah 23:5-6
3   John 1:1-2
4   John 14:11

our minds around since we live in a physical world, bound by time and space. Much too often, we try to understand the Trinity with our heads. God's name is holy. According to this Scripture, Jesus and God are one; therefore, Jesus' name is holy.

CHAPTER 4

Thy Kingdom Come, Thy Will Be Done in Earth As It Is in Heaven

AT THIS POINT, IT IS important to realize the historical context of this prayer. Theologians stress that many of the words in the Lord's Prayer can be found within formal Jewish prayers and that these particular words deal with the present age as well as the age to come. Some say that Jesus believed that a shift in the ages was happening in His ministry and that this prayer involved a petition for God to set this shift in motion as well as for God to rule in the individual lives of the people.

The age in which Jesus and His disciples lived was considered the evil age. They looked forward to the age to come, which is often called the "kingdom of God." During this kingdom, Satan will be defeated; and sin will be no more. By saying this portion of the prayer, we are expressing our belief that God will have the final victory over sin, thus creating an ideal existence.

Because of the depth of the Lord's Prayer, the request, "thy kingdom come, thy will be done," can refer to our present circumstances as well as our future. When we are held in the grip of some misguided passion, we long for a change that will release us from the grasp of sin. We pray for God's will to intervene in our imperfect lives, just as His will exists in the perfect state we know as Heaven. We long for cleansing and for our misdirected lives to shift out of the darkness and into a place of peace and comfort, where we feel useful and good.

Jesus continues to speak of the kingdom of God when He nears Jerusalem shortly before His triumphal entry. In Luke 19, Jesus uses the parable of the ten minas to teach His followers what they should do while they wait for the kingdom.[1] Luke explains in verse eleven that the people of Jerusalem think that the kingdom of God is going to come immediately, so Jesus tells the parable about a nobleman who gives ten minas to ten servants. (A *mina* was a sum of money equal to fifty shekels, which might be valued at or near $200 in U.S. currency today.) While the nobleman is absent, he expects his servants to be good stewards of his money and invest wisely. The servants did not earn this money. It does not belong to them; but because of their admiration, and possibly fear, of their master, they invest the money as best they can. However, one servant simply wraps his ten minas in a cloth for fear of losing them. When the master finds out that the servant has not invested, he takes the

---

1   Luke 19:11-27

money away from the servant and gives it to another who has invested wisely.

Much can be gleaned from this parable, but several lessons stand out. First, we must realize that all we have comes from God. When we realize that we are not *owners* but *caretakers* of our possessions, we are more likely to have a giving heart and to share with others. We are to be good stewards of our personal possessions. We can invest wisely by appreciating and caring for what we own and by helping those who are less fortunate. The ten minas refer not only to material possessions but also to our relationships as well. We are to appreciate and love each other so that God's love can flourish and spread. When we invest in love, the returns are great.

Next, Jesus is telling His followers that He is going to leave and prepare the kingdom. While He is absent, He expects His people to be good stewards of all that God has given them in this life. The kingdom of God can be considered the future as well as the present. Jesus teaches His disciples that He is going to prepare a place for them in the kingdom. Today, Christians look for the return of Christ and His kingdom.

We can also see the kingdom of God as God's presence in our lives or as an awareness of the Holy Spirit. When we stray from what God desires for us, we lose peace. Often, this loss is not because we have broken a list of rules and feel guilty; it comes from the face of God becoming distant and cloudy. We feel unrest because our days are being wasted. This should be the sign to stop, turn our face toward God, and pray. For anyone who feels this unrest in his soul, his passions in life have become misguided; and there is a lack of peace. He is not experiencing the kingdom of God.

Often when we pray, we do not honor God until the end of the prayer. We say something like, "in the name of Jesus. Amen." But first, we recite a list of requests that center on our wants. Jesus begins His prayer as a God-centered prayer. The Lord's Prayer begins with a focus on God and places God's desire for our lives as its central theme.

Jesus begins the Sermon on the Mount with "Blessed are the poor in spirit: for theirs is the kingdom of heaven."[2] Following this sermon, Jesus teaches the Lord's Prayer and says, "Thy kingdom come."[3] Later, in Luke, Jesus answers questions concerning the kingdom of God: "And when he was demanded of the Pharisees, when the kingdom of God should come, he answered them and said, The kingdom of God cometh not with observation: Neither shall they say, Lo here! or, lo there! for, behold, the kingdom of God is within you."[4] Jesus clearly says that the kingdom of God can be experienced within us. This occurs by having a changed heart. When we pray for God's kingdom, we receive a changed heart through the action of the Holy Spirit. These changes are reflected in how we live our daily lives and how we interact with others. This request for God to bring His Spirit upon us is an unselfish appeal so that we can express God's love to others.

---

2   Matthew 5:3
3   Luke 11:2
4   Luke 17:20-21

CHAPTER 5

Give Us This Day Our Daily Bread

HUNGER WAS A CURRENT THREAT in Jesus' day, just as it is today in many parts of the world. God supplies our food by blessing our land but also by giving us means by which we can provide for our families. People who live in agricultural communities see the direct connection between the field and the table. In the movie *Shenandoah*, Charlie Anderson prays the way that many of us feel about our lives, as well as our food: "Lord, we cleared this land. We plowed it, sowed it, and harvest it. We cook the harvest. It wouldn't be here and we wouldn't be eating it if we hadn't done it all ourselves. We worked dog-bone hard for every crumb and morsel, but we thank you Lord just the same for the food we're about to eat, amen."[1] The fictional character, Charlie Anderson, still clings to the idea that he and his family are responsible for the bounty they enjoy. In the Lord's Prayer, Jesus wants us to realize that everything we have is a gift from God.

---

1   *Shenandoah*, directed by Andrew V. McLaglen (1965: Universal City, CA).

Jesus intends for us to acknowledge that our food comes from God. We can also reason that if God supplies us with our bread, He will also satisfy all hunger within. Jesus refers to Himself in the Gospel of John as the Bread of Life: "For the bread of God is he which cometh down from heaven and giveth life unto the world."[2] Then He continues, "I am the bread of life."[3]

When God reveals His name to the world through Moses, he says, "I AM." God wants us to concentrate on today. Jesus says, "I *am* the bread of life"; therefore, God *is* the bread of life. The bread is for today. We are asking God to give us "this day our daily bread." God wants to fellowship with us this day—right now.

Our soul hungers for a relationship with the living God. Our spirit needs to be replenished daily, just as we strengthen our bodies by eating every day. Too often, we starve ourselves spiritually by ignoring our daily spiritual bread. We try to fill the hunger with other things. For many of us, we develop passions that are misguided when our souls are really crying out for the bread of life.

It is when our burdens crash down upon us that we need to spend quiet time with God. We also need to replenish our starving souls by reaching out to others and letting God's love flow through us, nourishing our own spirit as we tend to the needs of our neighbors. God's love is not meant to be static, stored up, or hidden. His love is dynamic. It is meant to be spread to everyone. Jesus says, "Ye are the light of the world. A city that is set on a hill cannot be

---

2   John 6:33
3   John 6:35

hidden. Neither do men light a candle, and put it under a bushel, but on a candlestick; and it giveth light unto all that are in the house. Let your light so shine before men, that they may see your good works, and glorify your Father which is in heaven."[4] Jesus wants us to be a light to our world on a daily basis.

Jesus also uses the analogy of bread to explain how the kingdom of God can spread. He tells the people a parable about bread-making: "The kingdom of heaven is like unto leaven, which a woman took, and hid in three measures of meal, till the whole was leavened."[5] The yeast increases the volume of bread. Since Jesus says, "I am the bread of life," He wants us to increase His love in the world.

It is here that the prayer makes a change from the word *thy* to the word *us*. The Lord's Prayer begins by focusing on God and His will for our lives. Now the prayer shifts the attention toward us but still keeps within the will of God. God cares about the things we need each day. Jesus is aware that it is very difficult for someone to concentrate on the spiritual when the physical is in need; therefore, Jesus has us address our physical needs before we begin praying for our spiritual ones. When people are hungry or thirsty or lacking the physical comforts of life, God cares.

When we pray this part of the Lord's Prayer, we are not praying a self-centered prayer. Jesus guides us to pray in such a way that shows we are aware of the struggles faced by others. This is evident

---

4   Matthew 5:14-16
5   Matthew 13:33

when He instructs us to pray, "Give *us* this day *our* daily bread" (emphasis mine), instead of "Give to *me* my bread." Theologians interpret this part of the prayer to mean that we are requesting everything essential for life—not just food and drink but health, home, relationships, and peace.

Notice that Jesus does not pray for tomorrow's bread or for bread throughout the year. There are three reasons for this omission. First, in Jesus's day, finding enough food for a day was a blessing. Jesus was speaking to the conditions of the people living in that region.

Next, praying just for today's food is a show of faith. During the Sermon on the Mount when Jesus gives the people the Lord's Prayer, He speaks to them about laying up earthly treasures: "Lay not up for yourselves treasures upon earth, where moth and rust doth corrupt, and where thieves break through and steal . . . For where your treasure is, there will your heart be also."[6] When we lay up treasures on earth, we are relying on our own strength and not the blessings that come from God. When trying to overcome compulsive behaviors, we must look toward God each day and accept His guidance and blessings *that* day and not look toward tomorrow.

The third reason that Jesus speaks of today's bread is because He wants us to rely on God and not on our own strength. In today's world—with our insurance policies, bank accounts, credit lines, and packed freezers—we store away enough food and cash to last

---

6   Matthew 6:19, 21

us for years. This self-reliant lifestyle often removes our daily need for God. This is not to say that we should empty our cupboards and checking accounts and go live on a mountaintop waiting for God to feed us. By asking God to "give us our daily bread," we are acknowledging an awareness that God meets our physical needs each day, and from this provision grows an appreciation and gratitude which blossom into proper stewardship of our gifts from God.

By asking for our bread on a daily basis, we guard against greed. When we store up treasures on earth, we not only forget where our blessings come from; but we also tend to want more. It is very difficult to know where to draw the line with material possessions. We always want one more closet or one more garage to store away the stuff of our lives.

When a parent places the cookie jar on a high shelf and controls how often the child can have a snack, the child not only is protected from the harmful effects of sugar and fat; but he also appreciates the parent's discipline when he finally gets a periodic treat. When we ask for our daily bread, we are acknowledging God's ability to protect us and do what He knows is in our own best interests. When we ask God for our bread daily, we are asking Him to ration our possessions so that we can avoid becoming insatiable gluttons. We are asking Him to help us see the material things of this world in a perspective that is pleasing to Him.

Jesus promises us that He will care for our spiritual hunger by comparing it to our physical needs: "I am the bread of life: he that cometh to me shall never hunger; and he that believeth on me shall never thirst."[7] Jesus provides us with this promise, but it is conditional. We must be willing to *come* and willing to *believe*.

In John's gospel, Jesus is in Jerusalem near the sheep gate pool, also known as the healing pool. It was a common belief in that day that when the water stirred, a person could be healed of his affliction if he were dipped into the pool. A man who had been an invalid for thirty-eight years was lying beside the pool. He had no one to help him enter the water. Jesus asked this man a very important question: "Wilt thou be made whole?"[8] This odd question may seem to have an obvious answer, but it is important enough for Jesus to ask it, anyway. Jesus wants to know if the man genuinely wishes to be healed. In reality, there are those among us who are satisfied wallowing in their self-pity. They are not willing to accept Jesus' offer and be healed of their misguided passions. They are not yet willing to *come* and *believe*. Jesus is not pushy. He will always ask. He will wait.

After the man answers, Jesus does not have to wait for the water in the pool to stir or for the man to be dipped into the pool. All Jesus asks is that the man have a willing heart and to obey His command: "Rise, take up thy bed, and walk."[9] Notice that Jesus did not simply say, "You are healed." He gave the man instructions on what he must do: "Get up! Pick up your mat and walk." This must have seemed impossible for a man afflicted for thirty-seven years.

---

7   John 6:35
8   John 5:6
9   John 5:8

It was important that the man put his faith into action. However, Jesus' command was not unreasonable. He did not say, "Pick up your mat and fly!" Jesus will always take us from where we are to where he wants us to be.

Compulsive afflictions can linger for years; and since they are such a private shame, we feel alone with no one to help. The Holy Spirit can heal us if we truly wish to be healed. We can feel the Spirit of Jesus asking our hearts, "Do you want to get well?" And if the answer is yes, then we must obey His command and walk away from our misguided passions and walk toward those who can aid us in our healing. God has placed many caring friends and family members in our lives. He also guides professionals who are knowledgeable in the cycle of addictions. But first, we must ask ourselves the most important question: do I want to get well?

From the very beginning of His ministry, Jesus has a clear vision of His mission on earth. When He states, "I am the bread of life," He knows that, eventually, this Bread will be broken for the sins of all mankind. When Jesus was in the Upper Room with His disciples, He knew that the end of His life on earth was near. The Scriptures tell us, "And as they did eat, Jesus took bread, and blessed, and brake it, and gave to them, and said, Take, eat: this is my body."[10]

When we ask God to give us our daily bread, we are showing that we wish to depend daily on God. Often, we promise God and ourselves that we will put an end to our destructive attitudes and habits, never returning to these activities and ways of thinking.

---

10   Mark 14:22

Then, when we do return, we feel terrible and unworthy. Not only have we have shown personal weakness, but we have also broken our promise to God. The result can be depression and a plummeting self-esteem, which can then continue to fuel even more destructive behaviors. Society tells us that we must be strong and handle these problems ourselves. We hear tired phrases like, "Have a stiff upper lip," or "Pull yourself up by your own bootstraps." Jesus is telling us just the opposite.

When we feel alone and broken, Jesus can comfort us. While He walked on earth, He was cast aside and abandoned. His body was broken; and while on the cross, He cried out, asking if even God had forsaken Him.[11] Often, in our misguided lives, we feel the same. We feel that no one understands us and that we have sunken so deeply into our passion that not even God can reach down and pull us out of our dismal condition. Jesus is telling us that we need God every day. We need His love and care to help us this very day. We need our daily bread to gain strength to follow God's will daily.

---

11   Matthew 27:46

CHAPTER 6

And Forgive Us Our Debts, As We Forgive Our Debtors

IMMEDIATELY FOLLOWING THE LORD'S PRAYER, the Gospel of Matthew continues with Jesus' thoughts about forgiveness. This is the only part of the prayer where Jesus makes direct comments: "For if ye forgive men their trespasses, your heavenly Father will also forgive you: But if ye forgive not men their trespasses, neither will your Father forgive your trespasses."[1]

We are to ask God for His forgiveness of our shortcomings in the same measure that we forgive others of their shortcomings. At the center of the theme of forgiveness is love—unselfish love, forgiving love. Jesus commands us to love our neighbor and to love ourselves—and to do this equally. In Mark 12, one of the teachers of the law asks Jesus what is the greatest commandment. Jesus responds by telling him that the first and most important commandment: "And thou shalt love the Lord thy God with all thy heart, and with all thy soul, and with all thy mind, and with all thy

---

1   Matthew 6:14-15

strength . . . And the second is like, namely this, Thou shalt love thy neighbour as thyself."[2] Here we find forgiveness threaded among love. In order to forgive someone, we must first love him in the same manner that we love ourselves. When we are in the throes of some compulsive behavior, we may not love ourselves. With no self-love, there is no room for truly loving God or others.

Being self-involved does not necessarily mean that we are full of self-love. If this is the case, we must concentrate on our love of God first, and then our love for ourself and others will follow. The apostle John writes in his first epistle, "If a man say, I love God, and hateth his brother, he is a liar: for he that loveth not his brother whom he hath seen, how can he love God whom he hath not seen?"[3] Both of these commandments are connected. It is impossible to love only God and not love your neighbor or to truly love your neighbor and not love God.

Does this mean that someone who does not believe in God cannot love? Of course, they can love in a worldly sense. Our language is limited in its expressions of love. We say we *love* God, yet we also *love* chocolate cake. When we are connected to our Creator, His spirit of love and care for mankind flows from Him into us, where it cannot be contained. This spirit must then overflow to others.

We often think of love as an emotion only. In reality, love is an action. Love allows us to put someone's needs before ours,

---

2   Mark 12:30-31
3   1 John 4:20

regardless of whether or not we feel that this person is "worthy." When we see love this way, we are a little closer to understanding God's love for us.

God is our Creator; therefore, all of us have the ability to love, yet it is a love marked by condition. If we do not accept God, we have not accepted His love; therefore, God's gift of love and forgiveness has been rejected. It is only when we acknowledge our Creator and accept His forgiveness that we can properly channel His love to others.

Even though forgiveness is a condition of the heart, it can also manifest itself as an outward act. In the Lord's Prayer, Jesus speaks of forgiveness. He forgives His disciples even before they betray Him. Jesus' forgiveness of His disciples culminates in His taking the role of a servant and washing their feet in the Upper Room.

To be a servant for others does not mean that you are weak and down-trodden. Actually, to feel as if life is treating you badly is the opposite of service. When we feel lowly and worthless, we are concentrating on ourselves and not thinking about others. In order to serve effectively, we must find confidence in ourselves and in our abilities to serve and acknowledge that these skills come from God. Jesus is the ultimate Servant, yet it is difficult to imagine Jesus feeling inferior to others. While He walked on earth, Jesus was a man of confidence—a mission-minded individual. His mind was on the things of God. Forgiveness came from His heart and was displayed in His outward actions, making

Him the ultimate Servant. He tells his disciples, "But whosoever will be great among you, shall be your minister."[4]

The apostle Paul writes, "And be ye kind one to another, tenderhearted, forgiving one another, even as God for Christ's sake hath forgiven you."[5] God's gifts to His people cannot be counted, but the greatest gift is His forgiveness through His Son, Jesus Christ. Without God's forgiveness, our lives would be wracked with guilt. By requesting forgiveness, we are admitting to God that we live selfish lives and that we put our wants first. When we accept God's forgiveness, we are expressing to God that we intend to pass on His loving spirit to others in the form of forgiveness to all who have harmed us.

In the Lord's Prayer, Jesus does not recite a litany of sins, ordering them from greatest to least. He realizes that to be human is to trespass against God and others. Jesus first deals with our attitude toward God, and then He concentrates on our wrongdoing against our neighbors.

Forgiveness is just as essential to our spiritual growth as bread is to our physical well-being. The entire Bible demonstrates our broken relationship with God and His grace toward our rebellious nature. The results of our trespasses are separation from God and the loss of fellowship with Him. The request to be forgiven sheds light on the idea that we are not perfect. We put other things in the place of God. We hurt people and are hurt

4   Mark 10:43
5   Ephesians 4:32

by people. We need God to forgive us, just as we need to forgive others and ourselves.

For the person whose passions have gone awry, forgiveness of one's self is vital. Our secret shame often pushes us deeper into this dark hole because we do not feel forgivable. We think that our friends and family can never understand and forgive us; and certainly, we can never be forgiven by a holy God. We have covered ourselves in a cloud.

I believe the number one hurdle that a person who is stuck in the throes of an overwhelming, compulsive behavior must overcome is the thought that God is angry with him and that he is not good enough to be forgiven. But God *does* forgive. He forgives *totally.* Paul reminds us that God, speaking through the prophet Jeremiah, is able to truly forgive and forget: "For I will be merciful to their unrighteousness, and their sins and their iniquities will I remember no more."[6]

God forgives us for our misguided passions, but we must also be willing to forgive. We must find the strength to forgive ourselves and forgive others as well. Remember, no one has forced us into this habit, but life's situations can often direct us toward self-destructive behaviors. We must forgive anyone we feel has contributed to our habit or to our continued pursuit of our compulsion. They must be forgiven with the same measure that God has forgiven us. Jesus tells us, "And when ye stand praying,

---

6   Hebrews 8:12

forgive, if ye have ought against any: that your Father also which is in heaven may forgive you your trespasses."[7]

Forgiveness is especially difficult when the people we wish to forgive do not feel that they need forgiving. They do not see that they have done anything against us. It is much easier to forgive someone when that person admits he has hurt us. From the cross, Jesus cries out, "Father, forgive them; for they know not what they do."[8] This is the most difficult forgiveness. If the people had fallen to their knees, rent their clothing, and cried out for God to forgive them, Jesus' task would have been easier. But they did not. Instead, they hurled insults and cried, "Crucify him!" Still, Jesus forgave them. When people harm us, even if they do not recognize it or if they think they are in the right, we must find a forgiving heart.

By including this request for forgiveness in the Lord's Prayer, Jesus is telling us that forgiveness is ours *if we only ask*. We can lift the veil of shame by asking God to forgive us, and we must be willing to forgive ourselves and others.

---

7   Mark 11:25
8   Luke 23:34

CHAPTER 7

And Lead Us Not Into Temptation

WHAT IS TEMPTATION? WHERE DOES it come from, and why does Jesus wish for us not to be led there? According to *Merriam-Webster*, the word *tempt* is defined as "to entice to do wrong by promise of pleasure or gain."[1] The apostle James explains the origin of temptation: "Let no man say when he is tempted, I am tempted of God: for God cannot be tempted with evil, neither tempteth he any man: But every man is tempted, when he is drawn away of his own lust, and enticed."[2] This verse shows that temptation comes from our own desires and that falling into temptation is our responsibility. God does not lead us into temptation. Jesus says for us to ask for God to lead us *not* into temptation; therefore, we must pray for Him to lead us in another direction.

Jesus knows that when we yield to temptation, we take our eyes off God. The whole of temptation can be summed up quite

---

1   *Merriam-Webster*, s.v. "tempt," accessed July 12, 2023, https://www.merriam-webster.com/dictionary/tempt.
2   James 1:13-14

easily: we are tricked into believing that a particular activity or way of thinking will not interfere with our relationship with God or with other people in our lives. We have convinced ourselves that no harm is being done—or, at the very least, no one will find out. This misconception is one of the true dangers of our misguided passion. We begin to believe that our behavior is not harmful or that it is actually helping us in some way. We convince ourselves that our habit is no more than a harmless guilty pleasure, like eating an occasional piece of chocolate cake.

At this point, we begin to compare our problem behavior with other vices. The pornographer says that the human body is beautiful and is convinced that at least he is not drinking and driving or harming his body with cigarettes. The alcoholic explains that drinking calms his nerves and gives him the edge he needs so that he can remove the stresses in his life. He condones his activities by telling himself that at least he is not doing hard drugs. We can eventually get to the place where we do not even see our activities as temptations. We become hardened.

"Then spake Jesus again unto them, saying, I am the light of the world: he that followeth me shall not walk in darkness, but shall have the light of life."[3] When our path is illuminated, we can see the stumbling blocks. On a dark night, a flashlight does not shine all the way to the end of the walkway, but it shines on our feet directly in front of us so that we can clearly see the dangers and avoid them. The Holy Spirit does this for us spiritually by giving

---

3   John 8:12

us knowledge so that we can recognize temptation. If we have our hearts open to God, He will let us know the temptations that line our daily walk.

Too often, we are not satisfied with just knowing the path immediately in front of us. We want to see around the corner so that we can know tomorrow's temptations as well as tomorrow's blessings. Just as Jesus says for us to ask for our daily bread, He also wants us to ask God for enlightenment each day so that we may veer out of the harmful way of temptation.

For something to be a temptation, we have to recognize it as a temptation, since temptations can be different for everyone. When we ask God to "lead us *not* into temptation," we are asking Him for knowledge. We are asking Him to shine His light on our paths and expose the things in our lives that will cause us to stumble. We are asking Him to teach us what things will tempt us. If a man walks with God, there is no way that he can say, "I did not know that this was something that would hurt me." God will use the Holy Spirit to illuminate the stones that will trip us in our daily walk. When we walk with God, He will teach us.

Many times in the New Testament, Jesus is called Teacher. He teaches us not only what we should avoid but also what things are good and right. These lessons come through the Word of God. The psalmist recognizes God's Word as the light that illuminates our way: "Thy word is a lamp unto my feet, and a light unto my path."[4]

---

4   Psalm 119:105

"Lead us not into temptation" is a cry for God to help us resist temptation. We are asking God to make us aware of tempting circumstances and to give us the strength to walk away. Notice that Jesus does not ask us to pray, "Remove us from all temptation." Yes, God is all-powerful and can simply take away any temptations we may face; but because of God's total love for us, He has instituted free will into our world. If we ask, God will throw out a "red flag" to warn us of a temptation. He will also allow us a way out of the temptation, but He will not remove it. He simply casts His light on it so that we can recognize it for what it is.

The request "lead us not into temptation" is an admission that we are weak and need God's help. The apostle Paul admits to his weakness when he writes, "I find then a law, that, when I would do good, evil is present with me . . . O wretched man that I am!"[5] But in his letter to the Corinthians, Paul writes: "There hath no temptation taken you but such as is common to man: but God is faithful, who will not suffer you to be tempted above that ye are able; but will with the temptation also make a way to escape, that ye may be able to bear it."[6] When temptations arise, we should look for God's hand leading us out of the thoughts or actions that lure us. God will provide a very clear escape route if we are willing to open our eyes and hearts to Him.

The best way to understand the nature of temptation is to study how Satan tempts Jesus at the beginning of His ministry. Read the

---

5   Romans 7:21, 24
6   1 Corinthians 10:13

following passage from the Gospel of Matthew and notice two main strategies used by the devil:

> Then was Jesus led up of the Spirit into the wilderness to be tempted of the devil. And when he had fasted forty days and forty nights, he was afterward an hungred. And when the tempter came to him, he said, If thou be the Son of God, command that these stones be made bread. But he answered and said, It is written, Man shall not live by bread alone, but by every word that proceedeth out of the mouth of God. Then the devil taketh him up into the holy city, and setteth him on a pinnacle of the temple, And saith unto him, If thou be the Son of God, cast thyself down: for it is written, He shall give his angels charge concerning thee: and in their hands they shall bear thee up, lest at any time thou dash thy foot against a stone. Jesus said unto him, It is written again, Thou shalt not tempt the Lord thy God. Again, the devil taketh him up into an exceeding high mountain, and sheweth him all the kingdoms of the world, and the glory of them; And saith unto him, All these things will I give thee, if thou wilt fall down and worship me. Then saith Jesus unto him, Get thee hence, Satan: for it is written, Thou shalt worship the Lord thy God, and him only shalt thou serve. Then the devil leaveth him, and, behold, angels came and ministered unto him.[7]

---

7   Matthew 4:1-11

First, Satan does not lie to Jesus. The truth is much more enticing, especially if it is a twisted truth. Satan tempts the weak, hungry Jesus to turn stones into bread. Where is the lie? Jesus is truly the Son of God, and He has the power to turn the stones into bread.

The Gospels tell us that later in His ministry, Jesus turns water into wine at a wedding feast and on another occasion increases the fish and the loaves so that a multitude can be fed. Surely, turning stones into bread is within His ability. Jesus has been fasting in the wilderness for a long time, so who would blame Him if He produces food for Himself? Often, our temptations make sense because they are not born out of lies but out of deception and twisted truth. Jesus knows that it is not the time for Him to eat, so He resists the temptation by returning to God's Word and the complete truth.

The second strategy used by Satan is to take Jesus to the next level of temptation. Since Jesus has resisted His temptations by returning to the truths found in Scripture, Satan adopts a different strategy. "If thou be the Son of God, cast thyself down."[8] Then Satan quotes from the book of Deuteronomy, ramping up his temptation. He not only jabs at the truth by saying, "If you are the Son of God," but he uses Jesus' defense against Him by quoting Scripture.

When we are able to resist a particular temptation, we need to be even more on guard. The next assault will come at us with a vengeance. Jesus remembers this lesson at the end of His ministry.

---

8   Matthew 4:6

While in the Garden of Gethsemane, He tells Peter "Watch ye and pray, lest ye enter into temptation. The spirit truly is ready, but the flesh is weak."[9] Jesus knows what He is talking about because He has experienced Satan's tricks and He knows human nature.

Satan not only increases his method of temptation, but his enticement changes. The first temptation of Jesus is for personal comfort: to feed His hungry body. When Satan sees that Jesus is more interested in His ministry than in His own comfort, he changes his approach. The next two temptations deal with Jesus' ministry. He tempts Jesus to show the people that He is truly the Son of God and, finally, to have all the kingdoms on earth believe in the Son of God. We should not think of these temptations as being easy for Jesus to pass by. It is true that Jesus was sinless, but this does not lessen the temptations hurled upon Him. Being tempted is not a sin. Jesus' complete focus was on His ministry, so it stands to reason that His ministry was a target from Satan. Jesus' life, ministry, and death are rooted in His love for mankind; however, Jesus knows the temptation laid before Him is not the path that God wants Him to take; so with God's help, He is able to resist Satan.

If we expect that all temptations are born from lies, we are deceiving ourselves. Many of our temptations make sense to us. We can often turn to the Bible to support a twisted belief, just as Satan quotes Scripture to Jesus in the wilderness. This is why Jesus instructs us to ask for God's help and pray, "Lead us not into

---

9   Mark 14:38

temptation." After all, He knows how tough resisting temptation can be.

We must do our part to limit the temptation. Someone who has a problem with sweets cannot spend the day in a bakery. An alcoholic is asking for temptation if he always meets his friends in a bar. A person who has a compulsion toward pornography should block those websites or channels. We must be aware of the triggers that tempt us.

Counselors use the phrase, "Change your playgrounds and playmates." If the places you go or the people you socialize with present temptations to you, then it is time to consider a change in venue or friends. In order to make these changes, we must be able to recognize the temptations or "red flags" of our problem behavior. Jesus knows that it is easier to resist temptation before it has its hooks in us than to try to walk away after the temptation has begun. That is why we are to pray, "Lead us not into temptation." We are asking God to intervene *before* we are tempted. We pray that God will not only pull us from the depths of temptation but will also help us watch for the stumbling blocks in our path.

Again, remember what Jesus tells His disciples on the night of His arrest: "Watch and pray, that ye enter not into temptation: the spirit indeed is willing, but the flesh is weak."[10]

---

10   Matthew 26:41

CHAPTER 8

But Deliver Us from Evil (the Evil One)

EVIL EXISTS. WE DO NOT know why evil exists, but one fact is certain: it frightens us. We do not understand evil. We understand the relationship between poor choices and the consequences those choices bring, but the knowledge that a presence exists—a presence that desires nothing but our harm—shakes us to the core. We feel helpless; yet from life's uncertainty, faith is born. We are not defenseless against evil. God can protect us. If He were unwilling or unable, Jesus would not have included this petition in the Lord's Prayer. This is one area where we must be willing to turn everything over to God and simply trust Him. The presence of evil in the world is beyond our comprehension and our ability to counteract that evil. We must trust God and the Holy Spirit.

Jesus tells us, "In the world ye shall have tribulation."[1] The apostle Peter writes, "Be sober, be vigilant; because your adversary the devil, as a roaring lion, walketh about, seeking whom he may

---

1   John 16:33

devour."[2] In other words, we are tempted due in part to the devil and in part to our own lack of control. The good news that can be gleaned from this verse is that the tempter can be defeated if we are "alert and of sober mind." Jesus knows that for us to resist the devil's lies, we would need God's insight and love.

Too often, we do not want to accept that this part of the prayer may be referring to Satan. We want to consider evil happenings as situations created by mean-spirited people, not by an evil presence in the world; however, in this prayer, Jesus uses the masculine form of the word *evil*. It is the same form of the word He uses in the parable of the sower: "The tares are the children of the wicked one; the enemy that sowed them is the devil."[3] We cannot ignore the presence of evil or the evil one. The word *from* in the verse— "Deliver us from the evil one"—always refers to a person, rather than a situation.

The evil one is a master craftsman, and his tools are fear and temptation. He deceives us and introduces doubt and disbelief into our minds. He defeats us by giving us one of the most self-destructive attitudes: pride. Through pride, we begin to think that we are more important than our fellow man and that we do not need God. We can take care of ourselves. In fact, pride can make us feel that God actually *needs* us and that we are doing Him a favor by believing. Our pride distorts our thinking and puffs up our feeling of self-importance.

---

2   1 Peter 5:8
3   Matthew 13:38-39

Jesus speaks of temptation first and then of the evil one. He couples the phrase, "Lead us not into temptation" with "deliver us from evil." The evil in this world works through our desires and passions, misguiding us so that we turn our faces away from God. Jesus tells us that we have two adversaries: our own sinful nature and Satan.

We cannot simply blame all of our sins on the devil. The comedian Flip Wilson's female persona, Geraldine, made famous the classic excuse, "The devil made me do it." Satan does not *make* us do anything. Our own nature coupled with Satan's enticements leads us away from God's will. The evil one invites us into sinful attitudes and activities, but the choice to yield to his temptations is ultimately our own. Jesus tells us that God will help us defeat evil through our faith in Him.

Often, we feel that if we are not tempted to become involved in some activity that society considers sinful, then we have beaten the devil. After all, how can we sin if we are not tempted? Satan does not care whether or not we commit "social sins" or if we "behave badly," just as long as we remain far from the will of God. When our passions become misguided, we spend our time and energy on useless activities that remove our focus from God and His blessings. We turn from the face of God, and Satan is satisfied.

Engaging in some compulsion is a waste of our time and gives us a shameful heart so that we stop seeking God's will for our lives. The temptation to delve into these misguided passions is strong. Jesus knows our human heart. He knows that we do not possess the strength to resist. He knows that we need God's help. This is why we ask God to "lead" and "deliver us."

CHAPTER 9

For Thine is the Kingdom, and the Power, and the Glory, For Ever. Amen.

THIS LAST LINE OF THE Lord's prayer does not appear in the earlier Greek manuscripts but was added later. Are these the actual words of Jesus? No one really knows if Jesus closes the prayer this way or not. Either way, it is a phrase that many of us learned early in life, and it seems to be a fitting doxology to the Lord's Prayer.

The Old Testament never uses the phrase "kingdom of God"; however, it clearly demonstrates God's power over kings and kingdoms. Jesus uses the kingdom of God, often translated as "the kingdom of heaven," as a central theme in His teaching. In the Gospel of Mark, Jesus makes His purpose clear: "The time is fulfilled, and the kingdom of God is at hand: repent ye, and believe the gospel."[1] What does Jesus mean?

First, look at what Jesus does *not* mean. He is not speaking of a geographic kingdom or temple. He is not speaking of a political

---

1   Mark 1:15

structure or a race of people, or even the Church. The kingdom of God refers to God's rule. He invites people into the kingdom, but they are not the kingdom.

Jesus knows the kingdom of God will grow into something great from something very small. In Mark 4:30-32, He says, "Whereunto shall we liken the kingdom of God? or with what comparison shall we compare it? It is like a grain of mustard seed, which, when it is sown in the earth, is less than all the seeds that be in the earth: But when it is sown, it growth up, and becometh greater than all herbs, and shooteth out great branches; so that the fowls of the air may lodge under the shadow of it."

This parable describes the growth of the kingdom. Even the smallest act can grow. Do not allow yourself to be tempted not to do something because the task seems too large or because you do not feel equipped. Remember, you have the power of God at your disposal, whatever your circumstances.

Often, when we think of the power of God, we picture judgment and wrath raining down from Heaven on the guilty. God is not like the strict schoolmaster ready to wield His stick upon bad little boys and girls. He lovingly demonstrates His power to all of mankind in a way that appears incredibly humble. His power is displayed through His willingness to forgive. This is where the paradox is found. The single most powerful moment in history is when God, the Son, in the meek person of Jesus, humbles Himself to die on the cross. With this act of grace, God offers His power of forgiveness to the world through the resurrection of Jesus Christ. God sends His power to the weak in the form of the Holy Spirit.

Jesus entered into our world as a baby, the weakest and most humble of all humans. He grew up in a family that was economically depressed; and ultimately, He died the death of the shameful. God had to experience the weakness of being human in order to offer his power to all, and this power is manifested in forgiveness and love.

In his first letter to the Corinthians, Paul admits weakness: "And I was with you in weakness, and in fear, and in much trembling. And my speech and my preaching was not with enticing words of man's wisdom, but in demonstration of the Spirit and of power: That your faith should not stand in the wisdom of men, but in the power of God."[2] The power of the Holy Spirit can only work in us once we admit our weakness. The first step in breaking the chains of addictive behavior is to admit that we are powerless. It is God's power that tears the chains apart and releases us from this bondage so that we can work to glorify Him.

The glory of God refers to Divine honor. In the doxology at the end of the Lord's Prayer, God is given all honor and praise. This praise has never been so beautifully stated as in the words of the apostle John: "And the Word was made flesh, and dwelt among us, (and we beheld his glory, the glory as of the only begotten of the Father,) full of grace and truth."[3]

---

2   1 Corinthians 2:3-5
3   John 1:14

CHAPTER 10

A Prayer of Grace, Faith, Hope, Love, and Peace

THE LORD'S PRAYER IS BEAUTIFUL in its completeness. Through God's grace, this prayer underscores our faith and gives us hope. These words are a demonstration of God's love to all people and provide peace in times of turmoil.

Religions across our globe are packed with ways that people attempt to atone for their sins. For some, it is simply a matter of opening an earnest heart to God. Others require confession to a religious leader, while some beliefs teach self-deprivation and even mutilation of the body. All of this is for one purpose: an effort to obtain grace.

Grace is favor from God that is undeserved. In the Lord's Prayer, Jesus instructs us to say, "Give us this day our daily bread." He does not say for us to ask for bread only when we have worked for it. He did not indicate that we must act in any way to deserve this daily bread. In asking God to give it to us freely, with no strings attached, we are acknowledging His grace.

Conditional grace is a misguided theology. There are still people in our society who think they are quoting the Bible when they say, "God helps those who help themselves." This saying not only is absent from the Bible, but it is also totally unscriptural. It is a saying that teaches conditional grace, which does not exist. Conditional grace tells us that we must act in some particular way in order to win God's favor. Jeremiah 17:5 states, "Thus saith the LORD; Cursed be the man that trusteth in man, and taketh flesh his arm, and whose heart departed from the LORD." When we live by trusting in the words and ideals set down by man, we will always be disappointed. God's love has no conditions. His grace has no strings attached.

In the Lord's Prayer, when we ask God to forgive all of our trespasses, we are actually asking for grace. Jesus does not say for us to ask God to forgive only the actions and attitudes that we know about. Also, we are not asking God to forgive us only for the trespasses that we know we will never make again. We know in the depths of our hearts that we will fall again, but this is no reason to stop asking for forgiveness. God knows that we need forgiveness, even when we do not realize that we need it; but His grace is unconditional and large enough to cover our past, present, and future misgivings. There is no way that we can earn God's favor, yet He pours it out to us freely.

The remainder of the petition for forgiveness is our promise to God that we will attempt to show favor to others and forgive them when they wrong us. Just as God shows His grace to us, we are to show it to others, even if others are not aware of it or, in our eyes, are not deserving. This is the essence of grace.

Hope is a continual looking ahead toward the kingdom of God. When we anticipate an optimistic outcome of something in the present time, guided by God, we have hope. The Lord's Prayer embodies hope by the simple fact that we are praying to God. The initial address—"Our Father, who art in heaven . . . thy kingdom come"—demonstrates our hope for an eternal relationship with God.

In this prayer, we have expectations of God's continued protection. We ask God daily to provide us with the things we need for life as well as the strength to overcome temptations and evil. We have hope for our relationships with others by asking God's forgiveness and requesting that He anoint us with His power so that we may be able to forgive ourselves and others.

When someone is living with low self-esteem, hope needs to be an essential part of his life. Misguided passions can cause someone to lose connections with friends and family. Often, the church and community look down on a person's behavior to the point where he feels like an outcast. When hopelessness blankets a person, life is hard to manage. The raw truth is that we cannot always count on our community, church, or even our family and friends to stand beside us in difficult times. But the hope that comes only from God is steadfast, if we believe and wait. The apostle Paul speaks much of hope. Few men who follow Christ were persecuted as much as Paul. Even though his circumstances were often dire, he had hope. In his letter to the Romans, he writes, "But hope that is seen is not hope:

for what a man seeth, why doth he yet hope for? But if we hope for that we see not, then do we with patience wait for it. Likewise the Spirit also helpeth our infirmities."[4]

Through all of biblical history, the presence of God has generated fear and awe. Adam, Abraham, and Moses all trembled at the sound of God's voice. The shepherds cowered at the sight of the angels of the Lord on the night Christ was born, and Saul fell to his knees when he was confronted by Jesus on the road to Damascus. When God makes His presence known, people fear and believe. But for most of human history, God has not shown His face in such an overt manner. If He did, we would not need faith. People feel that if God were to show His face to mankind through some marvelous miracle, faith would follow. But as Frederick Buechner writes, "Faith in God is less apt to proceed from miracles than miracles from faith in God."[5]

"Our Father who art in heaven" are the words that begin the Lord's Prayer. This greeting is a statement of faith. In these opening words, we are admitting to God that we know He is somewhere we are not, yet the mere fact that we are praying demonstrates our faith and that our prayer will be heard.

One of the greatest paradoxes in the entire Bible is that of faith and works. God gives us laws to follow. No Christian would ever say that there is no moral code, yet we know that we can never be truly good and earn our salvation. It is when we surrender to God that true faith begins to mature. In his masterpiece *Mere*

---

4   Romans 8:24-26
5   Frederick Buechner, *Wishful Thinking* (New York: Harper Collins, 1973).

Christianity, C.S. Lewis states, "If what you call your faith in Christ does not involve taking the slightest notice of what He says, then it is not faith at all—not faith or trust in Him, but only intellectual acceptance of some theory about Him."[6]

The word *faith* can also be used to indicate our system of belief. The Christian faith comprises numerous subsets of beliefs that have spurred many a heated argument. When we look at Jesus' words in the Lord's Prayer, we understand that He does not direct us to be Catholic or Protestant. He brings out the most important doctrine of the Christian faith: love. When Jesus was asked which is the most important commandment, He replied, "And thou shalt love the Lord thy God with all thy heart, and with all thy soul, and with all thy mind, and with all thy strength: this is the first commandment. And the second is like, namely this, Thou shalt love thy neighbour as thyself. There is none other commandment greater than these."[7]

In the Lord's Prayer, Jesus again makes this point very clear. At the beginning of the prayer, we are instructed to address God as "hallowed" and to desire His will for all the earth, thus showing our love for God. The only petition in the Lord's Prayer that tells us how to deal with other people is when we ask God to help us "forgive those who trespass against us." This request shows our love for others. The faith that we practice must embody these two ideas: love for God and love for others.

---

6   C. S. Lewis, *Mere Christianity* (London: Geoffery Bles, 1952).
7   Mark 12:30-31

Another aspect of faith shown in the Lord's Prayer can be found in the words "Thy kingdom come, thy will be done." We demonstrate our faith when we tell God that we believe in His will for our lives, even at times when we cannot see it happening. If we allow "Thy will be done," even when we know that our passions have not been God-directed, we can have faith that we are forgiven and that His power and glory can work through us by loving others.

Each Sabbath, people all across the globe trek toward churches and various houses of worship. They fill the pews of small country chapels as well as the huge mega-churches of the city. Some stay home and watch preachers on television or listen to radio ministries and podcasts, while others find their temples in the forest and commune with God through the silence of nature.

Most likely, we attend church for a combination of reasons. One of the first reasons that people give for going to church is to worship God, to become closer to their Creator. The fellowship with other believers enriches their lives and provides them with support during personal tragedy as well as celebration during good times. There are those who attend services to atone for their sins and shortcomings and to receive guidance for the coming week. Some grew up with the church as a cornerstone of their community, and now they attend simply out of habit.

Our entire religious experience is a search. But what are we searching for? First, we need to ask what we really want out of life. It is not until we answer this question in all honesty that we will know what we are expecting from our faith. Many of us desire the financial security that comes from having a stable job. Also, our health and the well-being of our loved ones is one of life's priorities. Many of us need to feel the satisfaction that comes from a creative art, and still others desire to serve and help those less fortunate. Some people strive to find a true love and develop a life-long relationship. Most people desire a combination of all these and more. These desires are simply the products of a deeper longing. We all want peace. We crave the pure peace that quiets our minds and warms our soul. We often feel that if our life conditions were different, we could have this peace. If we only had that job or if only our health could improve or if we could be certain that our loved ones were safe and happy, then peace would follow.

True peace is a state of mind as well as a condition of the soul. The Bible teaches us that our outward situation does not provide us with lasting peace, nor does it prevent us from obtaining it. Take an example of the most extreme and horrendous hardship—slavery. Many find it odd that neither Jesus nor His disciples condemned the practice of slavery. Theologians explain that slavery was such an integral part of society in Jesus› time that to abolish it would bring on much bloodshed. But there is another reason. The teachings of Jesus, when accepted, provide a peace that no social condition can alter. The freedom a slave yearns for would not bring him lasting peace any more than the multitude of riches enjoyed by the slave's master would deliver peace to Him. Jesus teaches us in the Lord's Prayer how to transcend the conditions of this world and to seek a lasting peace.

Throughout all of human existence, man has sought an eternal peace. One of the most famous epitaphs found in countless cemeteries is "rest in peace." In the Lord's Prayer, Jesus speaks of the kingdom of Heaven and an eternal relationship with the hallowed Father. The hope of this eternity with God provides us with peace of heart.

The Lord's Prayer is a prayer of peace. In this prayer, Jesus covers every aspect of the human condition. Peace can be found for the single mother who struggles to provide for her children as well as the CEO of a large corporation who is concerned about the jobs of hundreds of employees. The elderly shut-in with no family or the college student confused about the path his life is taking can both find peace through the Holy Spirit. The prisoner who spends hours in a bleak cell and the father sitting next to a hospital bed clutching the hand of his sick child can both find inner peace, despite their desperate circumstances.

The truth is that peace is what our soul craves; yet as long as we live in the physical world with all of its pride, greed, and self-centered attitudes, pure and lasting peace will never be obtained. When our faith is strengthened, our hope for lasting, eternal peace is made strong. Jesus stands on the threshold of the physical and spiritual realms of this universe, and He understands the unrest we experience in this life. He gives us His teachings so that we might live our lives in a way that brings us closer to God and His unwavering love.

Student Study Guide

This can be used as an independent or small group study.

Introduction:

1 | What does it mean for someone to have a passion for something? What are some things that people can be passionate about?

2 | If our passions become misguided, how does that often make us feel?

3 | Why does prayer exist?

4 | Read Luke 11:1. Did the disciples ever learn to pray?

5 | Do you know The Lord's Prayer by heart? If so, when did you learn it?

6 | Read John 4:4-26. In what ways was the Samaritan woman considered lowly?

7 | How did Jesus make her special and give her purpose?

8 | What did God say to you through this section?

9 | What is the purpose of this book and the Lord's Prayer?

10 | What part of the introduction caught your attention?

11 | Why did this part of the introduction catch your attention?

Chapter 1: Our Father

1 | Why does Jesus say "Our"?

2 | How do you picture God in your mind?

3 | Read Luke 11:11-13. Describe the father in this story.

4 | What is the best way to honor God? Read John 5:22-23.

5 | What things often keep us from a full relationship with the Father?

6 | What things do we want from the Father?

7 | Read Psalms 139:7-10. What is the main theme of this passage?

8 | What did God say to you through this section?

Chapter 2: Which Art in Heaven

1 | What is your view of Heaven?

2 | Read John 14:1-3. How does Jesus describe Heaven to His disciples?

3| What happens in the Bible when people come face to face with God?

4 | Read Matthew 6:19-21. What does Jesus say about the things we treasure?

5 | Read Galatians 5:22. List the fruits of the Spirit.

6 | What did God say to you through this section?

Chapter 3: Hallowed Be Thy Name

1 | What is the name of God?

2 | Read Exodus 3:13-14. What name did God call Himself when Moses asked?

3 | Read John 14:11. How else has God reached out to the world?

4 | Why did God reach out to us by sending Jesus?

5 | What did God say to you through this section?

Chapter 4: Thy Kingdom Come, Thy Will Be Done, On Earth As It Is in Heaven.

1 | What is the kingdom of God?

2 | What kind of change do you long for in your life?

3 | Read the parable of the ten minas in Luke 19:12-27. What are some things we learn from this parable?

4 | What are some things we learn from this parable?

5 | What are some things in our lives that we can be good stewards of?

6 | What is the first line of the Lord's Prayer?

7 | Where in the Lord's Prayer do we start to ask God for something?

8 | Read Luke 17:20-21. Where does Jesus say the kingdom of God can be found?

9 | What did God say to you through this section?

Chapter 5: Give Us This Day Our Daily Bread

1 | Who are we praying for in this part of the prayer?

2 | When are we asking for God to give us our bread?

3 | Read John 6:32-35. According to this verse, Who is the Bread of Life?

4 | Read Luke 23:42-43. How did the Bread of Life provide hope for the future of this man?

5 | Read Matthew 5:14-16. What are some ways to satisfy our spiritual hunger daily?

6 | Read Matthew 13:33. How does Jesus use the idea of bread in this verse?

7 | What word comes after "give" in this part of the prayer?

8 | Read John 5:1-9. How can the "daily bread" that comes from God help heal us of our misguided passions? What question did Jesus ask this man in verse six?

9 | Read Mark 14:22. What does Jesus do with the bread?

10 | What did God say to you through this section?

Chapter 6: And Forgive Us Our Trespasses As We Forgive Those Who Trespass Against Us.

1 | What is this part of the prayer asking?

2 | Read Matthew 6:14-15. What word describes what these verses are about?

3 | Read Mark 12:28-31. What is the most important commandment?

4 | Read 1 John 4:19-21. Who does this verse say is a liar?

5 | Read and compare Ephesians 4:32 and Mark 11:25. How does Paul say we must forgive each other? According to the words of Jesus, when does God forgive us?

6 | Have you ever felt as if you were unforgivable by God or by other people?

7 | Read Luke 23:34. While on the cross, what does Jesus ask God to do?

8 | What did God say to you through this section?

Chapter 7: And Lead Us Not Into Temptation

1 | Read James 1:13-14. Where does temptation come from?

2 | What are the lies of temptation?

3 | How does God lead us into temptation?

4 | Read John 8:12. How does Jesus describe Himself?

5 | Read Psalm 119:105. What are we asking of God?

6 | Does God remove all temptations?

7 | Read Romans 7:21, 24-25. Why does Paul call himself "wretched"?

8 | Read 1 Corinthians 10:13. How does this verse show us a way out of temptation?

9 | Read Ephesians 6:10-11. Where does temptation originate?

10 | Read Matthew 4:1-7. Identify the strategies used by Satan to tempt Jesus in the wilderness.

11 | Read Matthew 16:21-23. How does Jesus resist Satan?

12 | Read Matthew 26:41. Who, besides Satan, is responsible for your temptations?

13 | What did God say to you through this section?

Chapter 8: But Deliver Us From Evil (the Evil One)

1 | Read 1 Peter 5:8. Does the evil one exist? Who does this verse say he is?

2 | What did God say to you through this section?

Chapter 9: For Thine Is the Kingdom, and the Power, and the Glory, For Ever. Amen.

1 | Read Mark 1:15. What does Jesus say is near?

2 | Read Mark 4:30-32. What does Jesus compare the kingdom of God to?

3 | Read John 1:14. Who is the Word?

4 | What did God say to you through this section?

Chapter 10: A Prayer of Grace, Faith, Hope, Love, and Peace

1 | In order to complete this study of the Lord's Prayer, list several ways that the Lord's Prayer is a prayer of each of the following:

- Grace

- Faith

- Hope

- Love

- Peace

Instructor's Guide

THIS SECTION IS DESIGNED TO promote discussion and provide answers for the Student Study Guide.

Introduction:

1 | What are some things that people can be passionate about?

Jobs, hobbies, relationships, drink, food, money, and exercise are examples of things that people can be passionate about.

2 | If our passions become misguided, how does that often make us feel?

Our misguided passions can lead us into feelings of shame and loss. We feel alone and judged by others. We even feel as if we do not deserve to be loved. It is in this darkness that God shines the brightest.

There are two basic types of shame: healthy shame and toxic shame. Healthy shame keeps us in line. It makes us feel badly about doing or not doing something, and we work toward correcting it. Toxic shame is when we tell ourselves negative messages that we are not worthy of love or anything good in life. We can feel that not even God can love us, and this can stop us from praying. This type of shame can lead us away from God and into self-destructive behavior.

3 | Why does prayer exist?

Prayer is communication with God. If God were not interested in the lives of His children, prayer would not exist. The fact that Jesus taught His disciples to pray shows us that prayer is real and that God wishes for us to pray.

4 | Read Luke 11:1. Did the disciples ever learn to pray?

Of course, they did; but mostly, they recited Jewish prayers. So, why did the disciples want Jesus to teach them to pray? The disciples saw the closeness that Jesus had with God. They had witnessed how heartfelt his prayers were. They wanted to be more like Jesus; and to do this, they knew they needed to be closer to God. That is the purpose of this prayer—to help the disciples come closer to God. By studying the words of Jesus, we can become closer to God. The whole of Christianity can be found in these words.

5 | Do you know the Lord's Prayer by heart? If so, when did you learn it?

Recite the Lord's Prayer. There is power in studying the Lord's Prayer but not simply in reciting it. The power comes from the heart-shift that can occur when we study these words and apply them to our lives. When we truly believe in something beyond ourselves, we tend to see life on a grand scale; and our individual problems become easier to deal with.

6 | Read John 4:4-26. In what ways was the Samaritan woman considered lowly?

The Samaritan woman was the lowest in society for several reasons:

- She was a Samaritan, despised by the Jews for being a mixed race.
- She was a woman, a second-class citizen.
- This woman was shunned by the other women because she was an adulterer.

7 | How did Jesus make her special and give her purpose?

- *He spoke to her.*
- *He asked to share her cup.*

- *Jesus allowed her to be the first person on record to whom He revealed that He was the Messiah.*
- *He looked past her misguided passions and gave her purpose. I pray that He gives you purpose as well.*

8 | What is the purpose of this book and the Lord's Prayer?

The purpose of this book is to unlock the teachings embedded in the Lord's Prayer and to guide readers to embrace Jesus' beautiful words so that anyone who struggles in the clutches of some unhealthy behavior may find peace and may redirect his misguided passions toward a more fulfilling life.

9 | What part of the introduction caught your attention?

Answers will vary.

10 | Why did this part of the introduction catch your attention?

Answers will vary.

Chapter 1: Our Father

1 | Why does Jesus say "our"?

He was talking about all of mankind—present and future. He was talking about you and me, as well as

*the disciples. His message is inclusive, not exclusive. He
wants to include everyone and exclude no one.*

2 | How do you picture God in your mind?

*Too often, we base our beliefs or unbelief on our vision
of some unscriptural picture of God. This affects how
we pray as well as how we believe. Too often, we see God
as some old man sitting among the clouds. We think of
him as "Santa" or as "911." We turn to Him when we
want something or when we are in trouble. It is possible
that the disciples thought this way about God when
they recognized the unique closeness that Jesus had to
the Father. Jesus used the term Abba, which to us would
be like saying "Daddy."*

3 | Read Luke 11:11-13. Describe the father in this story.

*He is approachable. He loves his children. Notice that
Jesus speaks directly to the fathers by saying, "Which of
you fathers" (emphasis mine). He wants what is best for
His children.*

4 | What is the best way to honor God? Read John 5:22-23.

Jesus uses the term Father *as a way to show honor to
God. This Scripture goes further by telling us that we
show honor to the Father by honoring the Son, Jesus. We
often feel that to honor God, we must follow a list of*

dos and don'ts. We become "rule followers" and strive to
simply warm a pew each Sunday at church. Jesus had a
new idea. In order to honor God, we must accept, believe,
and follow Jesus.

5 | What things often keep us from a full relationship with
the Father?

- *Shame, denial, feeling that God is far away and*
  unapproachable
- *Fear of judgment*
- *Compulsive and misguided behaviors.*

6 | What things do we want from the Father?

We want Him to lift us out of the darkness. We want
Him to lift us out of shame. We want to be loved. We
want to feel accepted by God. We want to know that we
will not be abandoned.

7 | Read Psalms 139:7-10. What is the main theme of this
passage?

God will never desert us. He is always present.

8 | What did God say to you through this section?

Answers will vary.

Chapter 2: Which Art in Heaven

1 | What is your view of Heaven? Read John 14:1-3. How does Jesus describe Heaven to His disciples?

He describes it as a mansion with many rooms. If God is in Heaven, how can He be with us? Heaven is a state of perfectness—perfect peace. Jesus is telling us that God is perfect.

2 | What happens in the Bible when people come face to face with God?

People recoil in fear. Jesus is also telling us that God is not available in the flesh. We would not be able to look upon Him. Also, by not seeing, we have to live by faith. Jesus is telling us that God is in a perfect "heavenly" state, yet He is also standing before the disciples in a non-threatening body as Jesus.

3 | Read Matthew 6:19-21. What does Jesus say about the things we treasure?

He tells us that what we treasure will be shown in our hearts.

4 | Read Galatians 5:22. List the fruits of the Spirit.

Love, joy, peace, forbearance, kindness, goodness, faithfulness, gentleness, self-control.

5 | What did God say to you through this section?

Answers will vary.

Chapter 3: Hallowed Be Thy Name

1 | What is the name of God?

YHWH (YAHWEH)

2 | Read Exodus 3:13-14. What name did God call Himself when Moses asked?

I AM. If you do not want anyone to know much about you, one of the last things you do is give him your name. By God giving the human race His name, He is reaching out to the world.

3 | Read John 14:11. How else has God reached out to the world?

He sent His Son, Jesus.

4 | Why did God reach out to us by sending Jesus?

There is such a great gap between the Holy Father and mankind. Jesus filled the gap. Jesus made God approachable.

5 | What did God say to you through this section?

Answers will vary.

Chapter 4: Thy Kingdom Come, Thy Will Be Done, on Earth As It Is in Heaven.

1 | What is the kingdom of God?

This part of the prayer is actually a request. We are asking for God's kingdom. It is an ideal existence. It is an age where Satan will be defeated and sin will be no more. This request can be both a desire for a change in the world as well as a personal change in us.

2 | What kind of changes do you long for in your life?

We long for:

- *God's will to intervene in our lives*
- *Direction and cleansing*
- *Peace and comfort*
- *To feel useful and good.*

3 | Read the Parable of the Ten Minas in Luke 19:12-27. What are some things we learn from this parable?

A mina was a sum of money equal to fifty shekels. While the nobleman was absent, he expected his servants to be good stewards of his money and invest wisely. The servants did not earn the money. It did not belong to them; but because of their admiration and possible fear of their master, they invested the money as best they could. However, one servant simply wrapped his ten minas in a cloth for fear of losing it. When the master found out that he had not invested, he took the money away from the servant and gave it to a servant who had invested wisely.

4 | What are some things we learn from this parable?

We must realize that all we have comes from God. When we realize that we are not owners but caretakers of our possessions, we are more likely to have a giving heart and share with others. Jesus expects His people to be good stewards of all that God has given to them. The ten minas refer not only to material possessions but also to our relationships as well. We are to appreciate and love each other so that God's love can flourish and spread. When we invest in love, the returns are great.

5 | What are some things in our lives that we can be good stewards of?

We can be good stewards of relationships and material possessions.

6 | What is the first line of the Lord's Prayer?

"Our Father, which art in heaven."

7 | Where in the Lord's Prayer do we start to ask God for something?

This prayer begins with God. It does not get to us until the middle. But we usually do not pray this way. We jump right in with a list of wants. God wants us to put things straight. He wants us to put them into proper order.

8 | Read Luke 17:20-21. Where does Jesus say the kingdom of God can be found?

It can be found within you.

9 | What did God say to you through this section?

Answers will vary.

Chapter 5: Give Us This Day Our Daily Bread

1 | Who are we praying for in this part of the prayer?

We are praying for ourselves and others. The prayer changes from "Thy" to "us." The beginning of the Lord's

Prayer is focused on God and His will for our lives. But Jesus knew that the physical needs as well as the spiritual needs of a person must also be met. This is why Jesus focuses on our physical needs here.

2 | How often are we to ask God to give us our bread?

Daily—"this day." Here the prayer is focused on the present. We are asking God to supply our needs. Jesus also uses the term "bread" because our food is something we need every day. We can store it up, but we still need to eat. We are never satisfied; our bodies hunger for more. Just as we need bread constantly, our souls need the spirit of Jesus constantly. We often try to feed this hunger with other things. This is when our passions become misguided. We use material possessions and possibly relationships to try to fill our spiritual hunger. It never lasts. Notice that Jesus does not ask for tomorrow's bread. There are three reasons for this:

- *He was speaking of His current day.*
- *Food was scarce.*
- *Finding enough to eat for that one day was a blessing.*

Praying just for today's needs is a show of faith. He does not say to ask for a truckload and a barn to store it in, just in case God decides not to bless us later this week.

Jesus knows our hearts. If we concentrate too much on having enough of anything, we take our eyes off God. As we saw in the last section, "For where your treasure is, there your heart will be also" (Matt. 6:21).

Jesus wants us to rely on God and not on our own strength. Jesus wants us to move away from a self-reliant life and more to a God-reliant life. This does not mean that we are never to work, prepare, or save. It means we are to acknowledge where all of our blessings come from and to be patient and not greedy for the things in this life. With this attitude of "our daily bread," we become proper stewards of what we do own, and we show gratitude to God for all we have.

3 | Read John 6:32-35. According to this verse, Who is the Bread of Life?

"I am the bread of life . . . " God told Moses His name when Moses spoke to the burning bush. He said "I AM." Here Jesus says, "I AM the bread of life." Jesus is for our present, yet He is also our Hope for the future. Jesus calls Himself "the Bread of Life." Here He gives us a promise that we will never be hungry or thirsty, but it has two conditions:

- *We must be willing to come to Him.*
- *We must be willing to believe.*

4 | Read Luke 23:42-43. How did the Bread of Life provide hope for the future of this man?

Our present circumstances are not always great. Jesus is with us in the present, yet He also gives us hope for the future. Look at the thief on the cross beside Jesus. His present was not too great, to say the least. Luke 23:42-43 tells us that Jesus gave hope to the man hanging with Him on the cross. So, the Bread of Life is for the present as well as hope for the future. The past is behind us. One part of our daily bread is daily hope.

5 | Read Matthew 5:14-16. What are some ways to satisfy our spiritual hunger daily?

- *Jesus wants us to reach out to others because love is not something we keep to ourselves.*
- *Jesus is telling us that He wants us to be a light to others on a daily basis.*

6 | Read Matthew 13:33. How does Jesus use the idea of bread in this verse?

Here Jesus explains how our love spreads. He uses the idea of yeast or leaven in bread. He speaks of the kingdom of Heaven. In the last section, we saw where Jesus told us that the kingdom of God can be found "within you" (Luke 17:21). This kingdom is not to stay within us, but it is to be spread—like yeast in bread making causes bread dough to rise and increase in volume.

7 | What word comes after "give" in this part of the prayer?

The word is us. *Here we see that Jesus changes from* Thy *to* us. *He switches the attention to us but only as it applies to the will of God. This tells us that God cares about our needs on a daily basis. This is not a selfish part of the prayer. We are not just praying for ourselves but also for others. He did not say, "Give* me *this day* my *daily bread." The words* us *and* ours *show us that we are praying for others as well as ourselves.*

8 | Read John 5:1-9. How can the "daily bread" that comes from God help heal us of our misguided passions? What question does Jesus ask this man in verse six?

"Do you want to get well?" seems like an odd question since the man had come to this pool many times. However, Jesus wanted to hear him proclaim that he wanted to be well and that he needed help. Even though there was a ritual at the pool, all Jesus needed to know was that the man had a willing heart and was willing to show enough faith to obey Jesus command.

When we are dealing with compulsive behaviors, we often keep our feelings to ourselves. One part of our daily need is to be healed. But Jesus will ask you, "Do you want to get well?" If the answer is yes, then He will provide each day a way to help strengthen us. We must not be impatient. This is part of our "daily bread."

9 | Read Mark 14:22. What does Jesus do with the bread?

Jesus has told us that He is the "Bread of Life." Here He is telling us that this "bread" must be broken for all mankind. When we feel that our lives are broken, Jesus reminds us that through His brokenness, we can have a full life because He is "our daily bread."

10 | What did God say to you through this section?

Answers will vary.

Chapter 6: And Forgive Us Our Trespasses As We Forgive Those Who Trespass Against Us

1 | What is this part of the prayer asking?

It is asking God for His forgiveness of our shortcomings in the same measure that we forgive others of their shortcomings.

2 | Read Matthew 6:14-15. What word describes what these verses are about?

Forgiveness—this is the only petition in the prayer where Jesus makes comments. Being able to forgive is one of the most important parts of the Christian faith. God knows how our hearts and souls are made. If we are not willing to forgive, we cannot have a heart that truly accepts the Holy Spirit. For God to forgive us, we must forgive.

3 | Read Mark 12:28-31. What is the most important commandment?

To "love the Lord your God with all your heart." This verse continues and tells us the second greatest commandment: "Love your neighbor as yourself." This is where we find forgiveness connected to love. This is the only way we can truly forgive: to have love for someone—a very difficult task.

This is the process that will get us there:

- *In order to forgive someone, we must first love him.*
- *In order to love someone, we must first love ourselves.*
- *In order to love ourselves, we must first love God.*

Loving God is the first step in loving ourselves and loving others and ultimately forgiving others.

4 | Read 1 John 4:19-21. Who does this verse say is a liar?

This passage says that those who claim to love God but hate their brother or sister is a liar. Loving others is an outward sign of loving God. How often do we see people who profess to be Christians, yet harbor so much hate? Loving and forgiving will show in how we treat people. Jesus forgave His disciples for betraying and turning from Him even before it happened. In the Upper Room, Jesus removed His outer garment and then proceeded to wash the feet of the disciples. Can we do something that personal and still have an unforgiving attitude? No, we cannot. Jesus' love and forgiveness showed itself in an outward action toward His disciples.

5 | Read and compare Ephesians 4:32 and Mark 11:25. How does Paul say we must forgive each other? According to the words of Jesus, when does God forgive us?

Paul says, "Just as Christ forgave you." Jesus tells us in the book of Mark to forgive anyone we hold something against so that God can forgive us. These verses mirror what Christ says in the Lord's Prayer: "Forgive us . . . as we forgive those who trespass against us."

6 | Have you ever felt as if you were unforgivable by God or by other people?

Our secret shame often pushes us deeper into the dark hole of guilt because we do not feel forgivable. One of the biggest hurdles that we must overcome is the feeling that God is angry with us. Remember, the fact that Jesus put this line in the Lord's Prayer is proof that He knows we make mistakes and that we will continue to make them. Jesus did not say, "Forgive us if we trespass." He knows how we are made and that we are bound to trespass against God, against our neighbors, and against ourselves.

7 | Read Luke 23:34. While on the cross, what does Jesus ask God to do?

Jesus asks God to forgive the people who are crucifying Him because they do not know what they are doing. Based on the verses we have read and based on the Lord's Prayer, Jesus must have already forgiven them and is now asking God to do so as well.

The most difficult people to forgive are those who do not think they need your forgiveness. Friends and family may look down on you. Society as a whole may shun you, not hire you, and not let you join their church or organization. This is reality. Is it right? No, it is not. But Jesus did not say to forgive people only when they admit to being wrong. These people may continue to persecute us, but we must find it in our hearts to forgive.

It is important as well to realize that love and forgiveness is a process that takes time and effort. It is a process of loving God, ourselves, and others. We should work at it daily. This can actually be part of "our daily bread"—to love just a little more and forgive just a little bit each day.

8 | What did God say to you through this section?

Answers will vary.

Chapter 7: And Lead Us Not Into Temptation

1 | Read James 1:13-14. Where does temptation come from?

The apostle James explains that God does not tempt us. We are tempted by our own desire. Evil indicates Satan. Jesus did not concentrate so much on why we are tempted but on what happens when we are—we take our eyes off God. Notice that in the Lord's Prayer, Jesus does not do any finger-pointing. He concentrates on the consequences of our actions and how it affects our relationship with God. Temptation can be summed up easily: we are being tricked into thinking that a particular activity or way of thinking will not interfere with our relationship with God or with other people. We have convinced ourselves of two things: no harm is being done, and no one will find out.

2 | What are the lies of temptation?

- *Our actions are helping us in some way: "Alcohol calms my nerves."*

- *This action is harmless: the pornographer says, "The human body is natural and beautiful."*
- *This is not as bad as something else: "At least, I'm not drinking and driving."*

We eventually get to the place where we do not recognize our actions as temptations.

3 | How does God lead us into temptation?

He does not! Jesus prays for God to lead us in another direction. We are going in the direction of temptation ourselves, and the Lord's Prayer is asking God to change our direction: to lead us not along the path of temptation. Show us another way.

4 | Read John 8:12. How does Jesus describe Himself?

He says, "I am the light of the world." When the path before us is illuminated, we can see the stumbling blocks in our way. Jesus will bring these temptations to light. Often, we have the problem of wanting God to reveal what is around the corner. We try to look too far ahead. When we do, we stumble over things right in front of us. This goes back to the request for our "daily bread." We need to be satisfied with God's guidance each day and not try to look too far into the future. When we look too far ahead, we not only stumble into the temptations that litter our path; but we also miss the blessings that line our daily journey. We do not need to look at tomorrow through the eyes of today. For example, when we are hiking a mountain trail, if we look too far ahead, we will trip over roots in front of us; and we will miss the delicate wildflowers growing along the side of the trail.

5 | Read Psalm 119:105. What are we asking of God?

We are ultimately asking God to give us knowledge so that we can recognize the temptations that are in our daily walk. We are asking Him to teach us what things tempt us. In order for God to lead us around and away from a temptation, we have to admit to recognizing the temptation and admit it to ourselves and God. In some cases, we may have to admit it to a professional counselor so that God can use that person to steer us along another path.

6 | Does God remove all temptations?

No, the Lord's Prayer does not say "remove us from all temptation." God could have created us like robots, where we would love Him and our fellow man and never have to deal with temptation or sin. But God gave us free will, which shows His total love for us. He loves us so much that He is willing to lose us rather than enslave us. The Lord's Prayer is asking for God to

*give us strength to resist temptations. We are asking
God to send up a "red flag" to get our attention when
we encounter temptation.*

7 │ Read Romans 7:21, 24-25. Why does Paul call himself
"wretched"?

*The apostle Paul recognizes that he is weak. Even the
mighty apostle Paul considered himself a sinful man.*

8 │ Read 1 Corinthians 10:13. How does this verse show us a
way out of temptation?

*God will not let you be tempted beyond what you can
bear. When we are tempted, God will provide us a way
out. But we must ask. This is why Jesus put this request
into the Lord's Prayer.*

9 │ Read Ephesians 6:10-11. Where does temptation originate?

*According to the apostle Paul, temptation is from
Satan, yet we are not defenseless. We have free will to
accept the temptation or reject it. So, temptation has
a dual nature. It is born out of Satan and kept alive by
our own desires.*

10 | Read Matthew 4:1-7. Identify the strategies used by Satan to tempt Jesus in the wilderness.

Satan does not lie to Jesus. The truth is much more enticing than a lie, especially if it is a twisted truth. Satan calls Jesus the Son of God and tempts Him to turn the bread to stones. But the truth is that Jesus is the Son of God. And Jesus has the power to turn the stones to bread. He has the power to provide His own "daily bread." There is nothing sinful about using His power to satisfy hunger and thirst. Later, we see Jesus turn water into wine and increase fish and loaves, but Jesus knows that this was not the time to reveal all of His power to mankind.

Satan increases his assault. Satan changes his method. The next temptation will be harder to resist. The first is a temptation for personal comfort. Now, Satan tempts Jesus by using His ministry, something more important to Jesus than His own personal comfort. Satan uses Jesus' own strategies against Him. Since Jesus quotes Scripture to ward off the temptations, Satan turns to the use of Scripture to tempt Jesus: "For it is written . . . " Not all temptations are born from lies. This can be very confusing.

11 | Read Matthew 16:21-23. How does Jesus resist Satan?

He confronts Satan head-on through Peter, and He exposes Satan's disguise. Peter has taken Jesus aside and begins to talk to Him in a way that, to Peter, makes sense. Jesus sees it for what it is and exposes it. Satan cannot stand to have his twisted truths exposed to the light. If we can see the temptations for what they are, Satan will flee.

12 | Read Matthew 26:41. Who, besides Satan, is responsible for your temptations?

You are. You must do your part to limit temptations. Jesus told His disciples that it is their responsibility to "watch and pray." It is our responsibility to watch for temptations and to change any situations that might be tempting for us. We need to change our playgrounds and playmates. If being around certain people or situations tempts us to do things we should not, we need to try the best we can to remove ourselves from those situations.

Jesus knows that it is much easier to resist temptation before it has its hooks in us. This is why He teaches us to pray, "Lead us not into temptation." We are asking God to intervene before we are tempted. We are asking Him to help us watch for stumbling blocks in our path.

13 | What did God say to you through this section?

Answers will vary.

Chapter 8: But Deliver Us from Evil (the Evil One)

1 | Read 1 Peter 5:8. Does the evil one exist? Who does this verse say he is?

> *Yes, the evil one exists. If he does not, why would Jesus have this request in the Lord's Prayer? The idea of an evil force scares us. This verse tells us to be "self-controlled and alert." By giving us the Lord's Prayer, Jesus teaches us that being close to God will defeat evil. When Jesus uses the word* evil *in the Lord's Prayer, He uses the masculine form of the word, which is used for a person. He is speaking of Satan, not just bad things in general.*
>
> *Satan does not always entice us to behave badly in a legal or social sense. His goal is simply to turn our attention away from God. He can take control of our desires and passions and misguide them so that we no longer think about God. When he has accomplished this goal, he has won.*

Chapter 9: For Thine Is the Kingdom, the Power, and the Glory, For Ever. Amen.

1 | Read Mark 1:15. What does Jesus say is near?

> *The kingdom of God is near. To understand what Jesus means, we need to look at what He does not mean. The kingdom of God is not the following:*

- *A geographic place or the temple*
- *A political structure*
- *A race of people*
- *The Church*

The kingdom of God is God's rule. Jesus invites people into the rule of God.

2 | Read Mark 4:30-32. What does Jesus compare the kingdom of God to?

Jesus compares the kingdom of God to a mustard seed—a tiny mustard seed. The parable of the mustard seed describes the growth of the kingdom. It also describes the good deeds we do. Even the smallest deed or act can grow into something wonderful. Do not be tempted not to do something just because it seems too large. Remember, the power of God is with us. We have the power of God at our disposal for good.

Too often, we want to know the future. We want to see around the corner; and when we cannot, we fear that we cannot work for God. We think we are not smart enough, or we do not have enough money or have the right talent. But if you are in God's will, His power will provide what you need to advance His kingdom.

3 | Read John 1:14. Who is the Word?

Jesus is the Word. Jesus entered the world in the meekest circumstances. He never owned much of anything, and He died the death of the shameful; yet God poured His glory out on Jesus. Through Jesus, we can experience the kingdom of God, the power of God, and the glory of God.

4 | What did God say to you through this section?

Answers will vary.

Chapter 10: A Prayer of Grace, Faith, Hope, Love, and Peace

1 | In order to complete this study of the Lord's Prayer, list several ways that the Lord's Prayer is a prayer of each of the following: (These answers are open-ended, personal responses.)

- *Grace*
- *Faith*
- *Hope*
- *Love*
- *Peace*

Bibliography

Buechner, Frederick. *Wishful Thinking*. New York: Harper Collins Publisher, 1973.

Church of England, The. "The Lord's Prayer." The Church of England online. Accessed August 9, 2023. https://www.churchofengland.org/our-faith/what-we-believe/lords-prayer.

Keble, John. *The Christian Year*. Edited by Henry Morley. Taiwan: Project Gutenberg, 2013. https://www.gutenberg.org/files/4272/4272-h/4272-h.htm.

Lewis, C. S. *Mere Christianity*. London: Geoffery Bles, 1952.

O'Neill, Eugene. *Thirst*. Bookyards Library to the World. Accessed July 12, 2023. https://quotefancy.com/quote/1349605/Eugene-O-Neill-Man-is-born-broken-He-lives-by-mending-The-Grace-of-God-is-glue.

Tagore, Rabindranath. *Gitanjali*. London: Macmillian and Co., 1913.

About the Author

CURT RICHARDS HAS SPENT THE last forty years as an educator in public schools and colleges. When not teaching or writing, Richards loves spending his time with his family, studying nature, and reading. In 2023, he released a book for teachers, *30 Insights for New Teachers to Thrive*. Information about Richards' books can be found at www.curtrichards.com.

Ambassador International's mission is to magnify the Lord Jesus Christ and promote His Gospel through the written word.

We believe through the publication of Christian literature, Jesus Christ and His Word will be exalted, believers will be strengthened in their walk with Him, and the lost will be directed to Jesus Christ as the only way of salvation.

For more information about AMBASSADOR INTERNATIONAL please visit:

www.ambassador-international.com
@AmbassadorIntl
www.facebook.com/AmbassadorIntl

Thank you for reading this book!

You make it possible for us to fulfill our mission, and we are grateful for your partnership.

To help further our mission, please consider leaving us a review on your social media, favorite retailer's website, Goodreads or Bookbub, or our website.

Like a chef who seasons the meal in such a way that the distinctive flavors of each element is enhanced, Brian Onken invites readers of *More Than a Clever Story* into an invigorating and fresh taste of what Jesus says in His parables. Reading each parable attentive to Jesus' own words and the context in which these stories are found, you'll hear the voice of the Savior in renewed ways. No longer will you think of His parables as clever stories, but you'll find them to be life-giving words from Jesus.

Every human heart longs to be truly known and deeply loved. Each person has a God-given longing for fulfillment and a sense of belonging that is met only in a relationship with God. But does God really want a relationship with you? Yes, and He demonstrates His desire for that over and over again in Scripture. *Constant Companion* shows readers how to get past feelings of unworthiness, unwillingness, and other distractions and how to listen to God's voice through the practices of meditation, prayer, and Scripture-reading.

Most of us know Who Jesus is and would admit He was a good and kind Teacher while here on earth. But He is so much more—He is our Savior and God and worthy of all our worship. Through an in-depth study into the book of Hebrews, Joshua West and Gary Wilkerson take apart each verse, drawing the reader to a closer look at the Man Who lived here on earth for a short time and then became our Sacrifice to save us from our sins and live with us eternally in Heaven with Him. If you are searching for something more from God, dive into this study and drink in the jaw-dropping beauty of our Jesus.